S0-ART-701

gift books by kimberly rinehart and georgia rettmer:

tapestry of joy ...a gift of friendship

colors of hope ...a gift of encouragement

published and distributed exclusively by

The C.R. Gibson Company, a division of Thomas Nelson, Inc.

by special arrangement with

♥ it takes two ♥

le sueur, minnesota.

Aug. 10, 2006

to:

from:

copyright © 1999 kimberly rinehart and georgia rettmer

all rights reserved

published by C.R. Gibson.® Norwalk, Connecticut 06856

C.R. Gibson® is a registered trademark of Thomas Nelson, Inc.

printed in the United States of America

GB671  ISBN 0-7667-5390-5

# colors of hope

... a gift of encouragement

written by kimberly rinehart

illustrated by georgia rettmer

The C.R. Gibson Company, Norwalk, Connecticut  06856

if i could,
i would plant you a garden
of rainbows
to soften your world
with the colors of hope.

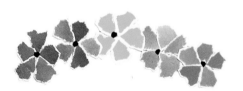

if i could,
i would wrap you
in warm summer breezes
to blow all the clouds of your worries away.

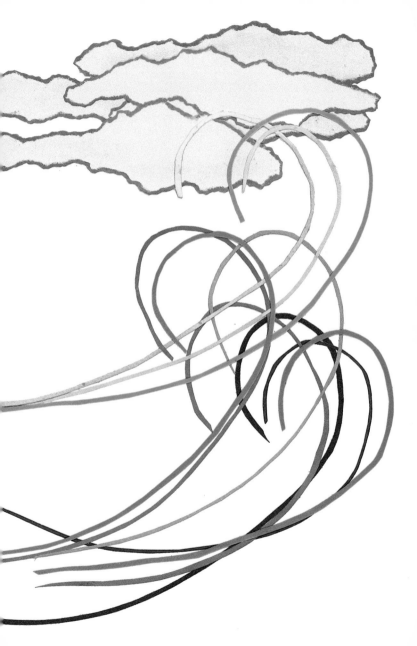

i would weave you
a memory
and paint you a sunset

and color your days
with the magic of spring.

i would bring you a songbird
to fill you with music

and sing you a story of laughter and love.

if i could,

i would clothe you in dreams
soft and peaceful,
and watch your tears melt
on the wings of a prayer.

i would carry your burdens
and share all that hurts you
and fill every moment of sadness

with joy.

if i could,
i would give you the strength
of a mountain,
the gift of a promise,
the faith
of a child . . .

for you are a special blessing
in every life you touch

and when your heart is heavy
i share your sadness too.

we have felt each other's joys
and we have shared each other's sorrows . . .

now may you feel the caring warmth
of being wrapped in borrowed strength.

if our hearts had known
no weeping,
how could they learn to laugh?

and if our souls had felt
no sorrow,
how would they ever grow?

when you touch the dark of night
the light of dawn will surely
find you.

when you let your spirit grieve
the joy of morning
will return.

you'll reach into your heart
and find a quiet song
of hope . . .

you'll think about tomorrow

and believe in all
that's true.

you'll look into your past
and see the colors
of a rainbow . . .

you'll remember how to laugh again
and love will calm
your fears.

you'll listen to your dreams
and hear them calling you
to follow . . .

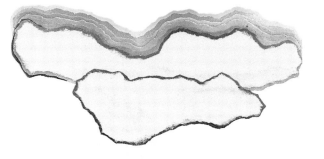

and faith will take your hand
while gently showing you
the way.

when the storm is finally over
i will still be here
beside you

hoping for the sunshine
to fall softly
on your path.

if i could,
i would bring you the promise
of healing
and show you the patience
to wait for the dawn . . .

and if only i could,

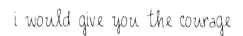

i would give you the courage

to place all your cares
in the palm
of God's
hand.